The Lord is my Shepherd

Edited by Juliet David
Illustrated by Julie Clay

CANDLE BOOKS

This simply worded version of the Twenty-third
Psalm has been specially written to introduce very
young readers to the best-loved psalm of David.

It follows closely the words of Scripture
in the Book of Psalms.

This book offers children helpful
first steps in devotions and prayer.

   J. D.

Lord,
you are my shepherd.

I have everything
that I need.

You let me rest
in green meadows.

You lead me beside
peaceful streams.

You give me new strength.

You guide me
along the right paths,
as you have promised.

Even when I walk
through the darkest valley,

I won't be afraid.
Because you are with me.

Your shepherd's rod
and shepherd's crook
help me feel safe.

You make a banquet for me,
while my enemies watch.

You welcome me
as your guest.
You fill up my cup
till it overflows.

Your goodness and love
will always be with me
– every day of my life.

Lord, I will live in your house forever.

BASED ON PSALM 23